*This book lists the 1984 Olympic gold medallists and the current Olympic records. Space is provided for **you** to record the 1988 champions. Use the official abbreviations given below and create your own souvenir of the 24th Olympic Games.*

AUS	Australia	FRA	France	MEX	Mexico
AUT	Austria	FRG	West Germany	NOR	Norway
BEL	Belgium	GBR	Great Britain	NZL	New Zealand
BRA	Brazil	GDR	East Germany	PAK	Pakistan
BUL	Bulgaria	HOL	Netherlands	POR	Portugal
CAN	Canada	HUN	Hungary	ROM	Romania
CHN	China	IND	India	SUI	Switzerland
CUB	Cuba	ITA	Italy	SWE	Sweden
DEN	Denmark	JPN	Japan	TCH	Czechoslovakia
ESP	Spain	KEN	Kenya	URS	Soviet Union
ETH	Ethiopia	KOR	South Korea	USA	United States
FIN	Finland	MAR	Morocco		of America
				YUG	Yugoslavia

Acknowledgments:
The publishers would like to thank the following people and organisations for their help in producing this book: Sandy Duncan and Garfield Blest (British Olympic Association); Geoff Cooke (British Cycling Federation); Mike Evans and Gavia Wilkinson-Cox (International Yacht Racing Union); Roger Hurt; F Miles (Joint Shooting Committee for Great Britain).
Photographs supplied by: Allsport — front cover bottom left and right, front endpaper, 4-9, 13, 14 left, 15 centre, 16, 22, 29, 32, 33, 35 bottom centre and right, 36-38, 41-49, 52, 54, 55, 58; George Herringshaw (ASP) — front cover top left and right, 3, 12, 14 centre and right, 15 left and right, 17-21, 30, 34 top, 39, 50, 53, 56, 59, back cover top right and bottom; Eileen Langsley — 34 bottom, 35 top and bottom left, 40, 51, back cover top left.
Based on an original manuscript by Bill Tancred.
Designed and illustrated by Chris Reed.
The publishers have made every effort to ensure that the information in this book was correct at the time of publication.

British Library Cataloguing in Publication Data

Olympics 88.
    1. Olympic Games, to 1988. For children
    I. Title
    796.4'8'09
    ISBN 0-7214-1085-5

First edition

Published by Ladybird Books Ltd Loughborough Leicestershire UK
Ladybird Books Inc Lewiston Maine 04240 USA

Printed in England

OLYMPICS 88

The ancient Olympic Games

The first recorded Olympic Games took place at Olympia in Greece in 776 BC. They were part of a religious festival held to honour the Greek god, Zeus.

The single event at the first meeting was a race along a track 192 m (630 ft) long. Later on other events were added, including wrestling, boxing, chariot racing and a pentathlon.

The first champions at these early Games were only awarded a crown of olive leaves. However, they were often rewarded with money by the people of their home town, who were grateful for an Olympic champion.

The ancient Olympic Games continued until AD 393, when they were abolished by the Romans, who had conquered Greece. The world then had to wait over 1,500 years to celebrate the Olympic Games once more.

A Greek statue of the discus thrower, Discobolos

The modern Olympic Games-
How it started

The world's greatest sporting spectacle was the idea of a French nobleman named Baron Pierre de Coubertin. During his travels round the world, Pierre de Coubertin was particularly impressed with the high interest in sports that he found in America and England.

It was after his travels that the Frenchman realised more than ever the truth of the ancient Greek ideal that the body, as well as the mind, must be cared for and improved.

He convinced many sporting authorities that an Olympic Games was an excellent means of teaching international understanding to the youth of the world. In 1896 the first Olympic Games of the modern era took place in Athens.

Pierre de Coubertin, founder of the modern Olympic Games

The start of the 100 m final in 1896

Olympic*Hall of Fame

1 *Johnny Weissmuller
(USA), winner of three gold
medals for freestyle swimming
and a bronze medal for water
polo (1924-1928)*
2 *Jesse Owens (USA), the most
successful athlete of the 1936
Games at Berlin*
3 *Bob Beamon (USA), whose
long jump record of 8.90 m
set in 1968 still stands*

*Throughout this book the terms Olympic(s) and Olympic Games refer to the Summer Olympic Games only, and not to the Winter Olympics.

3

4 Mary Peters (GBR), Olympic pentathlon champion in 1972
5 Mark Spitz (USA), winner of seven gold medals for swimming at the Munich Games. This is the record for the most victories at a single Olympic Games

This year's venue - Seoul, South Korea
September 17th - October 2nd

Previous Olympic venues and dates

I	1896	Athens	April 6-15
II	1900	Paris	May 20-October 28
III	1904	St Louis	July 1-November 23
*	1906	Athens	April 22-May 2
IV	1908	London	April 27-October 31
V	1912	Stockholm	May 5-July 22
VI	1916	Berlin	Not held owing to war
VII	1920	Antwerp	April 20-September 12
VIII	1924	Paris	May 4-July 27
IX	1928	Amsterdam	May 17-August 12
X	1932	Los Angeles	July 30-August 14
XI	1936	Berlin	August 1-16
XII	1940	Tokyo, then Helsinki	Not held owing to war
XIII	1944	London	Not held owing to war
XIV	1948	London	July 29-August 14
XV	1952	Helsinki	July 19-August 3
XVI	1956	Stockholm/ Melbourne	June 10-17 November 22- December 8
XVII	1960	Rome	August 25- September 11
XVIII	1964	Tokyo	October 10-24
XIX	1968	Mexico City	October 12-27
XX	1972	Munich	August 26- September 10
XXI	1976	Montreal	July 17-August 1
XXII	1980	Moscow	July 19-August 3
XXIII	1984	Los Angeles	July 28-August 12

*1906 Games held to mark the 10th anniversary of the modern games but not numbered since they were not held in the first year of the 1904-1908 Olympiad.

Note: Several countries did not take part in the 1984 Olympics in Los Angeles. Among those absent were the Soviet Union (URS), East Germany (GDR) and Bulgaria (BUL).

The 23 sports in 1988 Olympic Games

ARCHERY

Archery is probably the oldest sport in the world and is thought to have become an organised sport in the 3rd century AD.

The Olympic tournament features both individual and team events for men and women. In the preliminary round of the individual competition each archer must shoot thirty six arrows at a target placed at 90 m, 70 m, 50 m and 30 m in the men's competition and at 70 m, 60 m, 50 m and 30 m in the women's competition. The competitors with the highest scores progress through to the next round and at each stage of the competition, including the final, they shoot a further nine arrows from each of the set distances given above.

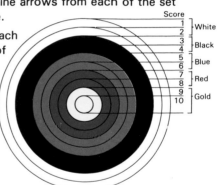

In the team event each member of the team of three shoots three arrows at a target placed at each of the four set distances.

The archery tournament will take place at the *Hwarang Archery Field.*

ARCHERY...RESULTS...

Event	1984 winner	1988 winner
Men		
Individual	D Pace (USA)	_____
Team	*New event*	_____
Women		
Individual	H-S Seo (KOR)	_____
Team	*New event*	_____

ATHLETICS

This is divided into **track** *and* **field** *events.*

Track events

The track is 400 metres per lap in all eight lanes. There are 'staggered' starting points for the 200 m, 400 m, 400 m hurdles, 800 m and the relays.

The 1,500 m is 3¾ laps; the 3,000 m and the 3,000 m steeplechase are both 7½ laps; the 5,000 m is 12½ laps; and the 10,000 m is 25 laps.

The 100 m, 100 m hurdles and 110 m hurdles are run on the straight.

The marathon starts and normally finishes in the athletics stadium and the distance is 42,195 m (26 miles and 385 yards.)

Events are timed using electronic apparatus which is correct to 1/100th of a second. This is how the official time is recorded for events up to and including 400 m.

OLYMPIC . . . Fred Lorz (USA) was disq... as winner of the marathon in . . when it was discovered that he ha... been given a lift in a car for part of the rac...

Great Britain's silver medal team in the 4 x 400 m relay at Los Angeles (Akabusi, Bennett, Brown and Cook)

Events from 800 m to 10,000 m are recorded to 1/10th of a second. The marathon is recorded to the whole second.

In starting an event, the starter's commands are 'On your marks' (in the starter's native language) and, for races up to 400 m, 'set.' As soon as the competitors are still, the pistol is fired. All competitors are allowed one warning for a false start and are disqualified for a second false start.

When finishing an event the winner is the first athlete to reach the finishing tape with any part of his or her *torso*. (This does not include the head, arms or feet.)

During the race itself, competitors must stay in their allocated lane (if any). Jostling and obstructing other competitors is not allowed. The track judges will disqualify athletes guilty of these offences.

Hurdles and steeplechase

There are ten *flights* in the four hurdle events. They are 1.067 m (3 ft 6 in) high for the men's 110 m, 0.91 m (3 ft) high for the men's 400 m and 0.84 m (2 ft 9 in) for the women's 100 m. For the women's 400 m event the hurdles are 0.76 m (2 ft 6 in) high. Hurdles knocked down unintentionally do not result in disqualification. This could however make the hurdler slower.

In the steeplechase event there are twenty eight hurdle barriers and seven water jumps.

1 Carl Lewis (USA), 100 m, 200 m and long jump Olympic champion (1984). He also won a gold medal in the 4 x 100 m relay

2 Ben Johnson (CAN), 1987 World champion at 100 m

3 Joaqhim Cruz (BRA), winner of the Olympic gold medal at 800 m in 1984

Men's events	Olympic record and time	1984 winner and time	1988 winner and time
100 m	J Hines (USA) 9.95	C Lewis (USA) 9.99	
200 m	C Lewis (USA) 19.80	C Lewis (USA) 19.80	
400 m	L Evans (USA) 43.86	A Babers (USA) 44.27	
800 m	J Cruz (BRA) 1:43.00	J Cruz (BRA) 1:43.00	
1,500 m	S Coe (GBR) 3:32.53	S Coe (GBR) 3:32.53	
5,000 m	S Aouita (MAR) 13:05.59	S Aouita (MAR) 13:05.59	
10,000 m	L Viren (FIN) 27:38.40	A Cova (ITA) 27:47.54	

4 Sebastian Coe (GBR) successfully defended his 1,500 m Olympic title in 1984

5 Said Aouita (MAR), World and Olympic champion at 5,000 m

6 Jack Buckner (GBR), European 5,000 m champion

4

5

6

Men's events	Olympic record and time	1984 winner and time	1988 winner and time
4 x 100 m relay	USA 37.83	USA 37.83	
4 x 400 m relay	USA 2:56.16	USA 2:57.91	
110 m hurdles	R Kingdom (USA) 13.20	R Kingdom (USA) 13.20	
400 m hurdles	E Moses (USA) 47.64	E Moses (USA) 47.75	
3,000 m s/chase	A Gärderud (SWE) 8:08.02	J Korir (KEN) 8:11.80	
20 km walk	*E Canto (MEX) 1:23:13	E Canto (MEX) 1:23:13	
50 km walk	*R Gonzalez (MEX) 3:47:26	R Gonzalez (MEX) 3:47:26	
Marathon	*C Lopes (POR) 2:09:21	C Lopes (POR) 2:09:21	

* These are best performance times since there are no records at these events

§ Best Olymp. performance

(Above) Ed Moses (USA), the most successful 400 m hurdler of all time

1 Tatyana Samolenko (URS), World champion at 1,500 m and 3,000 m
2 Silke Gladisch (GDR), 100 m and 200 m World champion
3 Ingrid Kristiansen (NOR), World champion 10,000 m runner

men's ents	Olympic record and time	1984 winner and time	1988 winner and time
00 m	E Ashford (USA) 10.97	E Ashford (USA) 10.97	_____
200 m	V Brisco-Hooks (USA) 21.81	V Brisco-Hooks (USA) 21.81	_____
400 m	V Brisco-Hooks (USA) 48.83	V Brisco-Hooks (USA) 48.83	_____
800 m	N Olizaryenko (URS) 1:53.43	D Melinte (ROM) 1:57.60	_____
1,500 m	T Kazankina (URS) 3:56.56	G Dorio (ITA) 4:03.25	_____
3,000 m	M Puica (ROM) 8:35.96	M Puica (ROM) 8:35.96	_____
10,000 m		New event	_____
4 x 100 m elay	GDR 41.60	USA 41.65	_____
4 x 400 m elay	USA 3:18.29	USA 3:18.29	_____
00 m urdles	V Komisova (URS) 12.56	B Fitzgerald-Brown (USA) 12.84	_____
00 m urdles	N El Moutawakel (MAR) 54.61	N El Moutawakel (MAR) 54.61	_____
larathon	§ J Benoit (USA) 2:24:52	J Benoit (USA) 2:24:52	_____

1 **2** **3**

Field events – throwing

A qualifying standard is set for all the field events. If athletes are successful at this stage, they proceed to the final. If fewer than twelve athletes qualify, the number is made up to twelve. The finalists in the four throwing events and in the long and triple jumps have three trials. The first eight, after three trials, earn three additional trials.

Weights of implements for the throwing events are as follows:

Shot	Discus	Javelin	Hammer
Men			
7.26 kg (16 lb)	2 kg (4 lb 6.55 oz)	800 g (28.22 oz)	7.26 kg (16 lb)
Women			
4 kg (8 lb 13 oz)	1 kg (2 lb 3.27 oz)	600 g (21.16 oz)	No women's event

Field events — jumping

In the **long jump**, the take-off board is 200 mm wide. A failure (red flag) arises if the jumper touches the ground, or makes an impression on the Plasticine beyond the far edge of the take-off board. The jump is measured from the take-off line to the nearest break in the sand made by any part of the body, including the limbs.

The **triple jump** is also known as the **hop, step and jump**. The rules are similar to the long jump except in the hopping phase. The athlete must land on the same foot as his or her take-off foot and in the 'step', land on the other foot. The trailing leg must not touch the ground.

Keith Connor (GBR), bronze medallist in the 1984 Olympics, showing the three phases of the triple jump — the hop, step and jump

In the **high jump** and **pole vault** events, two or more athletes often tie for first place by clearing the same height. If a tie exists, the winner is the competitor with the fewest failures at that height.

If a tie still exists, the winner is the athlete with the fewest failures at lower heights. After this, a tie is only broken for first place, in which case competitors have one attempt at the height at which they were unsuccessful. If no decision results, then the bar is lowered and raised accordingly until the tie is broken and a winner is declared.

(Opposite) *Fatima Whitbread (GBR), World champion javelin thrower*

FIELD EVENTS..RESULTS..

Men's events	Olympic record and result	1984 winner and result	1988 winner and result
High jump	G Wessig (GDR) 2.36 m	D Mogenburg (FRG) 2.35 m	
Long jump	R Beamon (USA) 8.90 m	C Lewis (USA) 8.54 m	
Pole vault	W Kozakiewicz (POL) 5.78 m	P Quinon (FRA) 5.75 m	
Triple jump	V Saneyev (URS) 17.39 m	A Joyner (USA) 17.26 m	
Shot	V Kiselyev (URS) 21.35 m	A Andrei (ITA) 21.26 m	
Discus	M Wilkins (USA) 67.50 m	R Danneberg (FRG) 66.60 m	
Hammer	Y Sedykh (URS) 81.80 m	J Tiainen (FIN) 78.08 m	
Javelin	M Nemeth (HUN) 94.58 m	A Haerkoenen (FIN) 86.76 m	
Decathlon	D Thompson (GBR) 8,797 pts	D Thompson (GBR) 8,797 pts	

1 Sergey Bubka (URS), World champion pole vaulter and the first man to vault over 6 m

2 Patrik Sjöberg (SWE), World champion at high jump

3 Daley Thompson (GBR), winner of the decathlon in the 1980 Olympics, successfully defended his title in 1984

Women's events	Olympic record and result	1984 winner and result	1988 winner and result
High jump	U Meyfarth (FRG) 2.02 m	U Meyfarth (FRG) 2.02 m	
Long jump	T Kolpakova (URS) 7.06 m	A Stanciu (ROM) 6.96 m	
Shot	I Slupianek (GDR) 22.41 m	C Losch (FRG) 20.48 m	
Discus	E Jahl-Schlaak (GDR) 69.96 m	R Stalman (HOL) 65.36 m	
Javelin	T Sanderson (GBR) 69.56 m	T Sanderson (GBR) 69.56 m	
Heptathlon	G Nunn (AUS) 6,390 pts	G Nunn (AUS) 6,390 pts	

4 Jackie Joyner-Kersee (USA), World champion long jumper and heptathlete

5 Stefka Kostadinova (BUL), World champion high jumper

6 Heike Drechsler (GDR), World record holder at 200 m and long jump

BASKETBALL

In the preliminary rounds of this competition the teams are divided into two groups. Each team plays every other in the same group, and gains 2 points for a win and 1 point for a loss. In the men's competition the four teams from each group with the highest number of points go forward to the quarter-finals, while in the women's competition the top two teams from each group go on to the semi-finals. At this stage the tournament is organised on a knock-out basis.

BASKETBALL...RESULTS...

	1984 winner	*1988 winner*
Men	USA	_____
Women	USA	_____

22

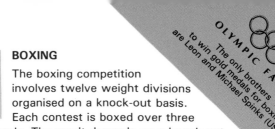

The only brothers to win gold medals for boxing are Leon and Michael Spinks (USA).

BOXING

The boxing competition involves twelve weight divisions organised on a knock-out basis. Each contest is boxed over three 3-minute rounds. The result depends on a knock-out, the referee stopping the contest for the safety of the loser, or on a points decision.

Many Olympic boxing champions, including George Foreman, Joe Frazier and Cassius Clay (later known as Muhammad Ali) have gone on to win world professional titles.

The venue for the boxing competition will be the *Chamshil Students' Gymnasium* (below).

Virgil Hill (USA), being defeated by Joon-Sup Shin (KOR)

BOXING...RESULTS...

Division	1984 winner	1988 winner
Light flyweight (48 kg)	P Gonzales (USA)	
Flyweight (Under 51 kg)	S McCrory (USA)	
Bantamweight (Under 54 kg)	M Stecca (ITA)	
Featherweight (Under 57 kg)	M Taylor (USA)	
Lightweight (Under 60 kg)	P Whitaker (USA)	
Light welterweight (Under 63.5 kg)	J Page (USA)	
Welterweight (Under 67 kg)	M Breland (USA)	
Light middleweight (Under 71 kg)	F Tate (USA)	
Middleweight (Under 75 kg)	J-S Shin (KOR)	
Light heavyweight (Under 81 kg)	A Josipovic (YUG)	
Heavyweight (Under 91 kg)	H Tillman (USA)	
Super heavyweight (Over 91 kg)	T Biggs (USA)	

CANOEING

In the Olympics there are two types of canoeing: kayaks and Canadian. In kayak canoeing the canoeist uses a paddle with a blade at each end. The canoeist must use the left-hand blade on the left side and the right-hand blade on the right side of the kayak alternately, making a twisting and rolling movement with the body.

The Canadian paddle has one blade, which is used on each side of the canoe alternately. Occasionally this type of canoeing is performed in a half-kneeling position for better propulsion.

The canoeing events will take place at the *Han River Regatta Course*.

CANOEING...RESULTS...

Men's events	1984 winner	1988 winner
500 m		
Kayak singles (K-1)	I Ferguson (NZL)	
Kayak pairs (K-2)	NZL	
Canadian singles (C-1)	L Cain (CAN)	
Canadian pairs (C-2)	YUG	
1,000 m		
Kayak singles (K-1)	A Thompson (NZL)	
Kayak pairs (K-2)	CAN	
Kayak fours (K-4)	NZL	
Canadian singles (C-1)	U Eicke (FRG)	
Canadian pairs (C-2)	ROM	
Women's events		
500 m		
Kayak singles (K-1)	A Andersson (SWE)	
Kayak pairs (K-2)	SWE	
Kayak fours (K-4)	ROM	

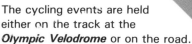

OLYMPI...
The longest cycling ra...
Olympic Games was in 191...
the course covered 320 km (199 m...

CYCLING

The cycling events are held either on the track at the **Olympic Velodrome** or on the road.

The 1,000 m time trial is held on the track. Competitors start off individually at intervals and the winner is the cyclist who records the fastest time over the course.

The individual sprint races cover three laps of the track and are usually contested by two or three cyclists. The winner is the cyclist with the fastest time over the last 200 m of the course, the earlier parts of the race being used to gain a favourable position.

In the 4,000 m individual pursuit race two cyclists start at opposite sides of the track. The aim is to catch up with the opponent and if this occurs the race is over. If a competitor does not manage to catch his opponent then the cyclist who records the fastest time is the winner.

The 4,000 m team pursuit involves teams of four cyclists, who compete as in the individual pursuit. Each member of the team takes it in turn to act as a pacemaker. The times of the first three cyclists in each team determine the winner.

The points race takes place over 150 laps of the track. On every 5th lap the first cyclist over the winning line gains 5 points, the second cyclist gains 3 points, the third cyclist gains 2 points and the fourth gains 1 point. The points awarded on the 75th lap and the final lap are worth double. The winner is the cyclist gaining the greatest number of points overall.

The road events are the 100 km team time trial for men, the road race for men (covering approximately 197 km) and the road race for women (covering 82 km).

The victorious Australian 4,000 m pursuit team in 1984 ▷

Men's events	1984 winner	1988 winner
Sprint	M Gorski (USA)	_____
1,000 m time trial	F Schmidtke (FRG)	_____
100 km time trial	ITA	_____
4,000 m individual pursuit	S Hegg (USA)	_____
4,000 m team pursuit	AUS	_____
50 km points race	R Ilegems (BEL)	_____
Road race	A Grewal (USA)	_____
Women's events		
Sprint	*New event*	_____
Road race	C Carpenter-Phinney (USA)	_____

EQUESTRIAN SPORTS

Equestrian sports include individual and team competitions in show jumping, dressage and the three day event.

OLYMPIC FACTS
Because of the strict quarantine laws in Australia, the equestrian events in the 1956 Games had to be held in Stockholm, not Melbourne.

The events will take place at the *Seoul Equestrian Park*, the *Wondang Ranch* and the *Olympic Stadium*.

Show jumping

In the individual event competitors must jump twelve to fifteen obstacles in two qualifying rounds. The maximum height of the obstacles is 1.60 m (5ft 3in) and the maximum width is 2.20 m (7ft 2½in). Competitors with the lowest number of faults progress to the final competition, where they must jump a further two courses.

In the team event the four members of each team tackle a course similar to that in the qualifying rounds of the individual events. The twelve teams with the fewest faults then jump against the clock over six obstacles up to 1.70 m (5 ft 6¾ in) in height. Only the three best scores for each team count towards the final result.

Dressage

Dressage judges the understanding between a horse and its rider. The competition involves a variety of paces, halts, direction changes, movements and figures. Points are awarded for each skill, out of a maximum of ten. In the team competition only the scores of the three best members count towards the team score. The twelve riders with the highest scores are then allowed to take part in the individual event.

Three day event

This includes dressage, show jumping and a cross-country endurance test. The scores of the three best members are added together to give the team total.

Lucinda Green (GBR), on Regal Realm in 1984

EQUESTRIAN...RESULTS...

Event	1984 winner	1988 winner
Show jumping		
Individual	J Fargis (USA)	_____
Team	USA	_____
Dressage		
Individual	R Klimke (FRG)	_____
Team	FRG	_____
Three day event		
Individual	M Todd (NZL)	_____
Team	USA	_____

FENCING

The fencing competitions include both individual and team events for men and women. Men fight with three weapons: foil, épée and sabre. Women fight with the foil only.

To score, the fencer must hit certain target areas on the opponent's body. The target areas are different for each weapon. In the qualifying rounds a fencer must score five hits to win. In the later rounds men must score ten hits and women eight hits. Each bout has a time limit.

The venue for the fencing tournament will be the *Olympic Fencing Gymnasium.*

Wires attached to each competitor electronically record hits to the target area

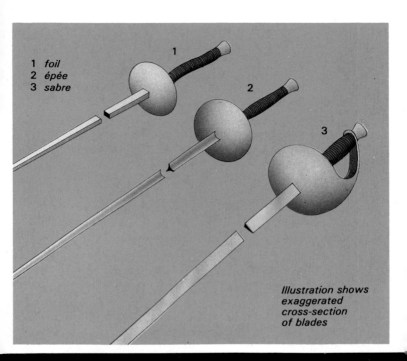

1 *foil*
2 *épée*
3 *sabre*

Illustration shows exaggerated cross-section of blades

FENCING...RESULTS...

Men's events	1984 winner	1988 winner
Individual foil	M Numa (ITA)	_____
Team foil	ITA	_____
Individual sabre	J-F Lamour (FRA)	_____
Team sabre	ITA	_____
Individual épée	P Boisse (FRA)	_____
Team épée	FRG	_____
Women's events		
Individual foil	J Luan (CHN)	_____
Team foil	FRG	_____

FOOTBALL (Association)

Only sixteen teams contest the medals at the Olympic Games in this sport. The teams are divided into groups of four with each team playing one match against each of the other teams in the group. The teams are awarded 2 points for a win, 1 point for a draw and no points for a defeat. The two teams in each group with the highest number of points qualify for the quarter-finals. The competition then becomes a knock-out tournament to decide the medal placings.

Players in the games *must* be amateurs, although many Olympic footballers have gone on to become well known professionals.

FOOTBALL...RESULTS...

1984 winner	1988 winner
FRA	

GYMNASTICS

There are eight events in the men's competition: floor exercises, pommel horse, rings, horse vault, parallel bars, horizontal bar, individual combined exercises and men's team. All competitors are given a mark out of ten for their performance in each of the events.

In the women's competition there are seven events: horse vault, uneven (asymmetric) bars, balance beam, floor exercises, individual combined exercises, women's team and rhythmic gymnastics. Again, all competitors are marked out of ten.

The gymnastics competitions will take place at the *Gymnastics Hall* at the *Seoul Olympic Park* (below).

Men's events	1984 winner	1988 winner
Floor exercises	Li Ning (CHN)	_____
Pommel horse	Li Ning (CHN) P Vidmar (USA)	_____
Rings	K Gushiken (JPN) LI Ning (CHN)	_____
Horse vault	Y Lou (CHN)	_____
Parallel bars	B Conner (USA)	_____
Horizontal bar	S Morisue (JPN)	_____
Combined exercises	K Gushiken (JPN)	_____
Team competition	USA	_____

2

1 Bilozertsev (URS), performing floor exercises

2 Bart Conner (USA), gold medallist for the parallel bars 1984

3 Yuri Korozen (URS)

4 Ecaterina Szabo (ROM)

5 Romania – team champions in 1984

6 Lori Fung (CAN)

7 Mary Lou Retton (USA)

3

1

GYMNASTICS...RESULTS...

Vomen's events		1988 winner
Iorse vault	E Szabo (ROM)	
Ineven bars	Ma Yanhong (CHN) J McNamara (USA)	
alance beam	S Pauca (ROM) E Szabo (ROM)	
loor exercises	E Szabo (ROM)	
hythmic competition	L Fung (CAN)	
ombined exercises	M-L Retton (USA)	
eam competition	ROM	

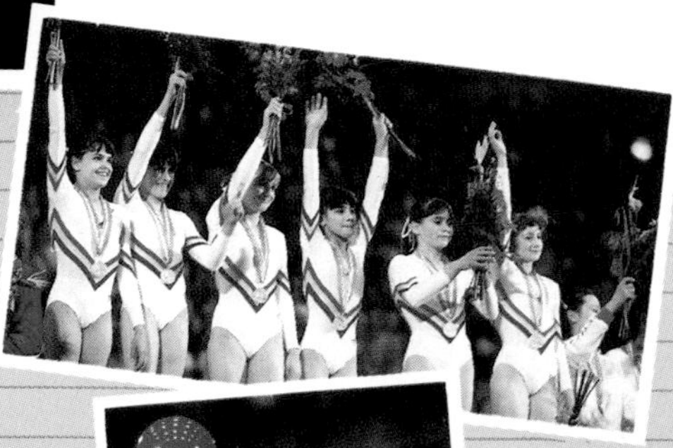

5

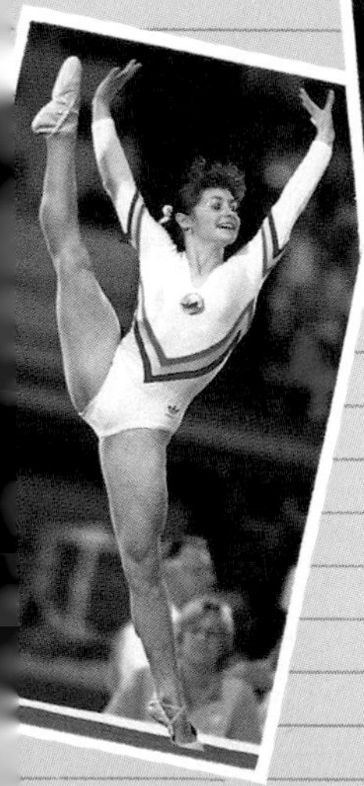

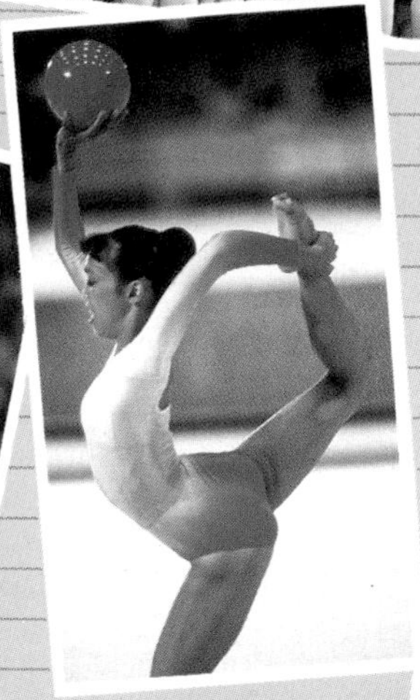

6

7

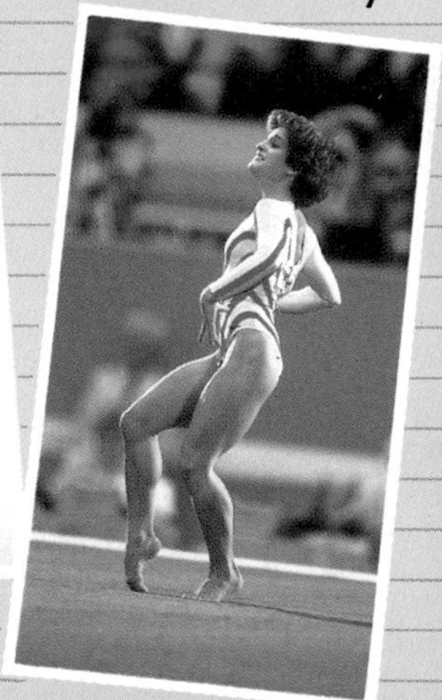

HANDBALL

Handball is a team game in which the player holding the ball is allowed to take three steps before he or she must either bounce the ball with one hand or pass it to another team member. Once the ball has been caught with two hands the player must either shoot at goal or pass the ball within three seconds. A goal is scored by throwing the ball past the keeper into the goal. Shots at goal must be made from outside the goal area.

HANDBALL...RESULTS...

	1984 winner	1988 winner
Men	YUG	_____
Women	YUG	_____

HOCKEY

The game of hockey is played between two teams with eleven players in each team.

In the Olympic tournament the teams are divided into two pools and the two top teams from each pool go through to the semi-finals. The event then becomes a knock-out competition.

Each match is played over two halves which each last for 35 minutes. At the semi-final and final stages of the tournament a match that has been drawn at the end of full-time will then have extra time played. If a draw still exists then the match is decided by penalty shots.

The hockey tournament will take place at the *Songnam Stadium*.

HOCKEY...RESULTS...

	1984 winner	1988 winner
Men	PAK	_____
Women	HOL	_____

Great Britain's bronze medal winning hockey team at the Los Angeles Games

JUDO

The sport of judo began as a means of self-defence. To be successful at this sport the *judoka* must be well balanced, fast and strong.

The competition is organised on an elimination basis. To win a bout outright a competitor must throw his opponent cleanly onto his back or immobilise him on the ground for 30 seconds.

The venue for the judo competitions will be the *Changchung Gymnasium* (below).

JUDO...RESULTS...

Weight class	1984 winner	1988 winner
Up to 60 kg	S Hosokawa (JPN)	_____
Up to 65 kg	Y Matsuoka (JPN)	_____
Up to 71 kg	B-K Ahn (KOR)	_____
Up to 78 kg	F Wieneke (FRG)	_____
Up to 86 kg	P Seisenbacher (AUT)	_____
Up to 95 kg	H-Z Ha (KOR)	_____
Over 95 kg	H Saito (JPN)	_____

MODERN PENTATHLON

When the seventeenth Olympic Games in ancient Greece finished, the war-like Spartans complained that there was not a competition that tested the all-round ability of the athletes. To answer this complaint a pentathlon was introduced at the next Games. The five events in the ancient pentathlon were discus, long jump, javelin, running and wrestling.

The five events in the modern pentathlon are show jumping (over fifteen obstacles on a 600 m course), fencing (épée), swimming (300 m freestyle), shooting (pistol or revolver at 25 m) and cross-country running (4,000 m).

PENTATHLON...RESULTS...

Event	1984 winner	1988 winner
Individual	D Masala (ITA)	
Team	ITA	

The 1976 gold medallists in the team event.
Left to right: *Jim Fox, Adrian Parker, Danny Nightingale (GBR)*

ROWING

The Chinese were the first to engage in the sport of long-boat racing on rivers and tidal waters. To this day Chinese festivals include races between dragon boats or shallow draft boats, 22 m (73 ft) long, moved by twenty seven oarsmen.

To standardise the events and equipment, many obstacles had to be overcome. This sport has probably made more progress in equipment than any other sport and it is extremely difficult to keep the competition athletic rather than technological.

No Olympic records exist for this sport as water conditions vary so much from one Games to another.

The rowing events will take place at the *Han River Regatta Course.*

Great Britain's coxed fours team, who won the gold medal in 1984

The gold medal winners of the double sculls in 1984

ROWING...RESULTS...

Event	1984 winner	1988 winner
Men (2,000 m)		
Single sculls	P Karppinen (FIN)	
Double sculls	USA	
Coxless pairs	ROM	
Coxed pairs	ITA	
Coxless fours	NZL	
Coxed fours	GBR	
Quadruple sculls	FRG	
Coxed eights	CAN	
Women (2,000 m)		
Single sculls	V Racila (ROM)	
Double sculls	ROM	
Coxless pairs	ROM	
Coxed fours	ROM	
Quadruple sculls	ROM	
Coxed eights	USA	

SHOOTING

The shooting tournament has a number of separate events for men and women and two open events where men and women compete together.

The open events are the skeet and Olympic trap shooting. In both cases competitors use a shotgun and fire at saucer-shaped clay targets. These targets are designed so that their flight is similar to that of a game bird at take-off. The 'game birds' are released from traps on the shooter's command. A hit is scored when the clay is visibly broken or reduced to dust.

In the running game target competition the target is shaped like a running boar and divided into ten rings. It is moved at a constant speed across an opening 10 m in width. Two speeds are used: a *slow run* where the target is shown for 5 seconds and a *fast run* where it is shown for 2½ seconds.

The shooting events will take place at the **Taenung International Shooting Range.**

The simple trap shown in the inset gives an idea of how the 'game bird' is fired into the air. It is used for both skeet and Olympic trap competitions

Matthew Dryke (USA)

42

Men's events	1984 winner	1988 winner
Rapid fire pistol (25 m)	T Kamachi (JPN)	_____
Free pistol (50 m)	H Xu (CHN)	_____
Air pistol (10 m)	*New event*	_____
Running game (50 m)	Y Li (CHN)	_____
Smallbore – **3 positions (50 m)**	M Cooper (GBR)	_____
Smallbore – **prone position (50 m)**	E Etzel (USA)	_____
Air rifle (10 m)	P Heberle (FRA)	_____
Women's events **Sport pistol (25 m)**	L Thom (CAN)	_____
Air pistol (10 m)	*New event*	_____
Air rifle (10 m)	P Spurgin (USA)	_____
Smallbore – **3 positions (50 m)**	X Wu (CHN)	_____
Open events **Trap**	L Giovannetti (ITA)	_____
Skeet	M Dryke (USA)	_____

Prone
position

Standing
position

Kneeling
position

SWIMMING

The swimmers compete using four different strokes: breaststroke, backstroke, butterfly and freestyle (usually the crawl). Medley races consist of each of the four strokes swum over four equal distances.

The fastest qualifying swimmer swims in the final in lane four (centre), the next quickest lane five, then three and so on. This explains the arrowhead formation when viewed on TV.

In the synchronised swimming competition for women there are both solo and duet events. Competitors must first complete six figures with various degrees of difficulty. They then perform a free routine to music lasting 3½ minutes in the solo event and 4 minutes in the duet event.

SWIMMING...RESULTS...

Men's events	Olympic record and time	1984 winner and time	1988 winner and time
Freestyle			
50 m		New event	_____
100 m	A Gaines (USA) 49.80	A Gaines (USA) 49.80	_____
200 m	M Gross (FRG) 1:47.44	M Gross (FRG) 1:47.44	_____
400 m	G Dicarlo (USA) 3:51.23	G Dicarlo (USA) 3:51.23	_____
1,500 m	V Salnikov (URS) 14:58.27	M O'Brien (USA) 15:05.20	_____
Backstroke			
100 m	J Naber (USA) 55.49	R Carey (USA) 55.79	_____
200 m	R Carey (USA) 1:59.99	R Carey (USA) 2:00.23	_____
Breaststroke			
100 m	S Lundquist (USA) 1:01.65	S Lundquist (USA) 1:01.65	_____
200 m	V Davis (CAN) 2:13.34	V Davis (CAN) 2:13.34	_____
Butterfly			
100 m	M Gross (FRG) 53.08	M Gross (FRG) 53.08	_____

Men's events	Olympic record and time	1984 winner and time	1988 winner and time
Butterfly			
200 m	J Sieben (AUS) 1:57.04	J Sieben (AUS) 1:57.04	_____
Individual medley			
200 m	A Baumann (CAN) 2:01.42	A Baumann (CAN) 2:01.42	_____
400 m	A Baumann (CAN) 4:17.41	A Baumann (CAN) 4:17.41	_____
Medley relay			
4 x 100 m	USA 3:39.30	USA 3:39.30	_____
Freestyle relay			
4 x 100 m	USA 3:19.03	USA 3:19.03	_____
4 x 200 m	USA 7:15.69	USA 7:15.69	_____

1 Victor Davis (CAN), winner of gold and silver medals for breaststroke

2 Michael Gross (FRG), winner of the 200 m freestyle and 100 m butterfly in 1984

SWIMMING...RESULTS...

Women's events	Olympic record and time	1984 winner and time	1988 winner and time
Freestyle			
50 m		New event	
100 m	B Krause (GDR) 54 79	N Hogshead C Steinseifer (both USA) 55.92	
200 m	B Krause (GDR) 1:58.33	M Wayte (USA) 1:59.23	
400 m	T Cohen (USA) 4:07.10	T Cohen (USA) 4:07.10	
800 m	T Cohen (USA) 8:24.95	T Cohen (USA) 8:24.95	
Backstroke			
100 m	R Reinisch (GDR) 1:00.86	T Andrews (USA) 1:02.55	
200 m	R Reinisch (GDR) 2:11.77	J De Rover (HOL) 2:12.38	
Breaststroke			
100 m	P Van Staveren (HOL) 1:09.88	P Van Staveren (HOL) 1:09.88	
200 m	L Kachushite (URS) 2:29.54	A Ottenbrite (CAN) 2:30.38	

1 Anne Ottenbrite (CAN)
2 Tracy Caulkins (USA)
3 Nancy Hogshead (USA) and Carrie Steinseifer (USA)
4 Petra Van Staveren (HOL)
5 Jolanda De Rover (HOL)

SWIMMING...RESULTS...

Women's events	Olympic record and time	1984 winner and time	1988 winner and time
Butterfly			
100 m	M Meagher (USA) 59.26	M Meagher (USA) 59.26	_____
200 m	M Meagher (USA) 2:06.90	M Meagher (USA) 2:06.90	_____
Individual medley			
200 m	T Caulkins (USA) 2:12.64	T Caulkins (USA) 2:12.64	_____
400 m	P Schneider (GDR) 4:36.29	T Caulkins (USA) 4:39.24	_____
Medley relay			
4 x 100 m	GDR 4:06.67	USA 4:08.34	_____
Freestyle relay			
4 x 100 m	GDR 3:42.71	USA 3:43.43	_____
Synchronised swimming			
Solo	No record	T Ruiz (USA)	_____
Duet	No record	USA	_____

4

5

47

DIVING

The diving competition consists of the springboard and platform (highboard) events.

The number of dives which each competitor performs is eleven for men's springboard, ten for women's springboard and men's platform and eight for women's platform.

Each dive is marked out of ten by the judges, based on how well the dive is performed. The highest and lowest marks are discounted and the remainder are added together and multiplied by a tariff value which varies according to how difficult the dive is.

(Right) *Five basic dives. All other dives are derived from these*

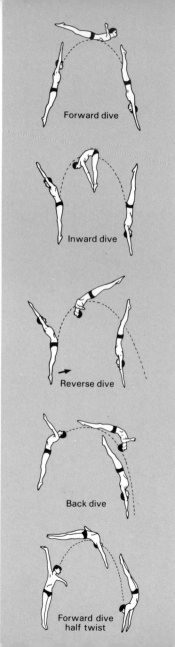

Forward dive

Inward dive

Reverse dive

Back dive

Forward dive half twist

Greg Louganis (USA), winner of both the springboard and platform events

Sylvie Bernier (CAN), springboard gold medallist

DIVING...RESULTS...

Men's events	1984 winner	1988 winner
Springboard	G Louganis (USA)	
Platform	G Louganis (USA)	
Women's events		
Springboard	S Bernier (CAN)	
Platform	J Zhou (CHN)	

WATER POLO

Water polo is a demanding team game played by two teams of seven players, one of whom is the goalkeeper. The game ..es place in a pool measuring a minimum of ⊃m x 25m x 1.80m deep (164ft x 82ft x 5ft 11in).

The game itself is divided into four 5-minute periods. The object of the game is to pass the ball and to throw it into the goal of the opposing team.

The twelve teams taking part in the competition are divided into two groups. Each team plays every other team in their group and the top two teams from each group then play in a knock-out competition to decide the medal winners.

WATER POLO...RESULTS...

	1984 winner	1988 winner
Men	YUG	

TABLE TENNIS

1988 will be the first year in which table tennis is included as an Olympic sport.

There are singles and doubles events for both men and women. The competitions are organised on a group basis for the first round. The highest placed players or pairs in each group then go on to compete in play-off matches to determine the final places.

Singles matches are the best of five sets and doubles matches are the best of three sets.

TABLE TENNIS...RESULTS...

Event	1988 winner
Men's singles	
Men's doubles	
Women's singles	
Women's doubles	

TENNIS

Tennis was part of the Olympic programme up until 1924 and then dropped until this year.

The tennis tournament consists of the following events: men's singles, men's doubles, women's singles and women's doubles.

OLYMPIC FACTS

The first female competitor to win an Olympic gold medal was Charlotte Cooper (GBR), who won the tennis competition in 1900.

New sport

Matches for men are the best of five sets and matches for women are the best of three sets. Tie-breaks operate in every set except the final one, where play must continue until one player or pair leads by two clear games.

The tennis matches will be played at the *Olympic Tennis Park, Seoul*.

Tennis was a demonstration sport at the 1984 Olympic Games held in Los Angeles. Steffi Graf (FRG) won the gold medal in the women's singles competition

TENNIS...RESULTS...

Event	1988 winner
Men's singles	
Men's doubles	
Women's singles	
Women's doubles	

VOLLEYBALL

This game involves six players in each team and is played on a court with a high net across the centre.

OLYMPIC FA

Between 1964 and 1980 the men's team from the Soviet Union won only 4 of its 39 matches and the women's team was defeated only twice in 28 matches.

The aim of the game is to return the ball over the net before it touches the ground. Each team may touch the ball up to three times before it must go over the net to the opposition. Points are obtained when the opposing team either hits the ball out of court or fails to return it before it touches the ground. Points are only given to the serving team and if the serving team is penalised the service then passes to the opposition.

Each match is the best of five sets. A set is won when a team gains 15 points with a 2 point lead.

The venues for this sport are the **Hanyang University Gymnasium**, the **Saemaul Sports Hall** and the **Chamshil Gymnasium**.

VOLLEYBALL...RESULTS...

	1984 winner	1988 winner
Men	USA	_____
Women	CHN	_____

WEIGHTLIFTING

OLYMPIC FACTS

Harold Sakata (USA) won the silver medal in the 82.5 kg class in 1948. He later starred as 'Oddjob' in the James Bond film Goldfinger.

The weightlifting competitors are divided into ten weight classes. Each competitor attempts to lift the heaviest possible weight using two different techniques: the *snatch* and the *clean and jerk*. Every weightlifter has up to three attempts at each weight and must succeed in lifting it before attempting a greater weight.

The winner is the competitor who successfully lifts the greatest total weight using both methods of lift. If two competitors tie, both having lifted the same weight, the competitor with the lightest body weight is declared the winner.

The competition will be held at the *Olympic Weightlifting Gymnasium*.

In the snatch, the competitor must lift the bar with both hands to arm's length above his head. This must be done in one continuous movement

WEIGHTLIFTING...RESULTS...

Weight class	Olympic record and result	1984 winner and result	1988 winner and result
Up to 52 kg	K Osmanoliev (URS) 245 kg	G Zeng (CHN) 235 kg	
Up to 56 kg	D Nuñez (CUB) 275 kg	S Wu (CHN) 267.5 kg	
Up to 60 kg	V Mazin (URS) 290 kg	W Chen (CHN) 282.5 kg	
Up to 67.5 kg	Y Rusev (BUL) 342.5 kg	J Yao (CHN) 320 kg	
Up to 75 kg	A Zlatev (BUL) 360 kg	K-H Radschinsky (FRG) 340 kg	
Up to 82.5 kg	Y Vardanyan (URS) 400 kg	P Becheru (ROM) 355 kg	
Up to 90 kg	N Vlad (ROM) 392.5 kg	N Vlad (ROM) 392.5 kg	
Up to 100 kg	O Zaremba (TCH) 395 kg	R Milser (FRG) 385 kg	
Up to 110 kg	L Tarenenko (URS) 422.5 kg	N Oberburger (ITA) 390 kg	
Over 110 kg	V Alexeyev and S Rakhmanov (both URS) 440 kg	D Lukim (AUS) 412.5 kg	

◁ *Nicu Vlad (ROM), gold medallist in the 90 kg weight class*

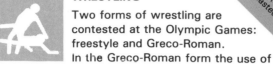

WRESTLING

Two forms of wrestling are contested at the Olympic Games: freestyle and Greco-Roman. In the Greco-Roman form the use of legs is restricted.

Each bout takes place on a 12 m (39ft 4¼ in) square mat and consists of two 3-minute periods. If both wrestlers have the same score at the end of this time the referee orders an extension of the bout until one wrestler scores a winning technical point.

The competition venue is the *Sangmu Gymnasium*.

Weight class	1984 winner	1988 winner
Freestyle		
Up to 48 kg (Light flyweight)	R Weaver (USA)	_____
Up to 52 kg (Flyweight)	S Trstena (YUG)	_____
Up to 57 kg (Bantamweight)	H Tomiyama (JPN)	_____
Up to 62 kg (Featherweight)	R Lewis (USA)	_____
Up to 68 kg (Lightweight)	I-T You (KOR)	_____
Up to 74 kg (Welterweight)	D Schultz (USA)	_____
Up to 82 kg (Middleweight)	M Schultz (USA)	_____
Up to 90 kg (Light heavyweight)	E Banach (USA)	_____
Up to 100 kg (Mid heavyweight)	L Banach (USA)	_____
Up to 130 kg (Heavyweight)	B Baumgartner (USA)	_____
Greco-Roman		
Up to 48 kg (Light flyweight)	V Maenza (ITA)	_____
Up to 52 kg (Flyweight)	A Miyahara (JPN)	_____
Up to 57 kg (Bantamweight)	P Passarelli (FRG)	_____
Up to 62 kg (Featherweight)	W-K Kim (KOR)	_____
Up to 68 kg (Lightweight)	V Lisjak (YUG)	_____
Up to 74 kg (Welterweight)	J Salomaki (FIN)	_____
Up to 82 kg (Middleweight)	I Draica (ROM)	_____
Up to 90 kg (Light heavyweight)	S Fraser (USA)	_____
Up to 100 kg (Mid heavyweight)	V Andrei (ROM)	_____
Up to 130 kg (Heavyweight)	J Batnick (USA)	_____

YACHTING

The regatta consists of seven different international classes. In six of these classes (Soling, Star, Flying Dutchman, Finn, Tornado and Division II), the crews can be made up of men or women. In the 470 class, men and women compete in separate events.

In each class there are seven races over a set course. The best six results from the seven races count towards the final medal placings.

The yachting events will be held on the waters of *Suyong Bay, Pusan.*

Flying Dutchman class, 1984

The United States team in the Star class

ЧACHTING...RESULTS...

Class	1984 winner	1988 winner
Open		
Soling (keelboat)	USA	_____
Star (keelboat)	USA	_____
Flying Dutchman (centreboard dinghy)	USA	_____
Finn (centreboard dinghy)	R Coutts (NZL)	_____
Tornado (catamaran)	NZL	_____
Division II (sailboard)	*New event*	_____
Men		
470 (centreboard dinghy)	*New event*	_____
Women		
470 (centreboard dinghy)	*New event*	_____

The 470 was a single open class event in 1984, when it was won by Spain

World records

Athletics – Track and Field*

Men's events	Record	Holder	Date
100 m	9.83	Ben Johnson (CAN)	1987
200 m	19.72	Pietro Mennea (ITA)	1979
400 m	43.86	Lee Evans (USA)	1968
800 m	1:41.73	Sebastian Coe (GBR)	1981
1,500 m	3:29.46	Said Aouita (MAR)	1985
5,000 m	12:58.39	Said Aouita (MAR)	1987
10,000 m	27:13.81	Fernando Mamede (POR)	1984
4 x 100 m relay	37.83	USA	1984
4 x 400 m relay	2:56.16	USA	1968
110 m hurdles	12.93	Renaldo Nehemiah (USA)	1981
400 m hurdles	47.02	Edwin Moses (USA)	1983
3,000 m st'chase	8:05.04	Henry Rono (KEN)	1978
20 km walk	1:18:40	Ernesto Canto (MEX)	1984
50 km walk	3:41:38	Raul Gonzalez (MEX)	1979
High jump	2.42 m	Patrik Sjöberg (SWE)	1987
Long jump	8.90 m	Bob Beamon (USA)	1968
Pole vault	6.03 m	Sergey Bubka (URS)	1987
Triple jump	17.97 m	Willie Banks (USA)	1985
Shot	22.91 m	Alessandro Andrei (ITA)	1987
Discus	74.08 m	Jurgen Schult (GDR)	1986
Hammer	86.74 m	Yuriy Sedykh (URS)	1986